...a people's theatre

THE ETIENNE SISTERS

by Ché Walker

with songs by Anoushka Lucas
additional songs by Sheila Atim

First performed at Theatre Royal Stratford East
on Thursday 10 September 2015

Cast

in alphabetical order

Bo	**Allyson Ava-Brown**
Ree	**Jennifer Saayeng**
Tree	**Nina Toussaint-White**
On piano	**Nikki Yeoh**
Duvivier	**Anthony Lennon**
Mother	**Jo Martin**

Creative Team

Written and directed by	**Ché Walker**
Songs by	**Anoushka Lucas**
Additional songs by	**Sheila Atim**
Designer	**Ti Green**
Musical Supervisor	**Anoushka Lucas**
Musical Director	**Nikki Yeoh**
Choreographer	**Patience James**
Lighting Designer	**Arnim Friess**
Video Designer	**Louis Price**
Sound Designer	**Sarah Weltman**
Casting Director	**Will Burton** for David Grindrod Casting
Singing Coach	**Rachel Bennett**
Assistant Director	**Greta Gould**

Production Team

Production Manager	**Ricky Parr**
Costume Supervisor	**Annelies Henny**
Company and Stage Manager	**Sarah Buik**
Deputy Stage Manager	**Kala Simpson**
Scenic Artists	**Mike Becket & Lizzie Wilkinson**
Set Construction	**Factory Settings**
Wardrobe Maintenance	**Holly Parr**

Thanks to

National Theatre

Cast biographies

Allyson Ava-Brown
Bo

Theatre credits include: Martha Reeves, *Dusty* (Charing Cross Theatre), Nina, *In Bed* (Theatre Centre Works), Kitten, *Snakes and Ladders* (UK tour), *Jack and the Beanstalk, Crowning Glory, Beauty and the Beast* (Theatre Royal Stratford East), Kimberley, *Snakes and Ladders* (Soho Theatre, Nightingale Theatre), Martha Sullivan, *The Swallowing Dark* (Theatre 503, Everyman Playhouse Studio, Best Actress nominee, Offie Awards), *London Road* (NT Studio), *Julius Caesar, The Tempest, Antony and Cleopatra* (RSC, Stratford, tour, West End), *Joyce Lane, Simply Heavenly* (Trafalgar Studios), *Georgina Big, The Villains Opera* and *Honk* (National Theatre), *Fantine, Les Misérables* (Queen's Theatre).

TV credits include: *Doctors, Casualty, Holby City, EastEnders* (BBC1), *Beatrice* (series lead), *Bear Behaving Badly, The Wrong Door, Sea of Souls, Kerching!* (BBC), *Secret Diary of a Call Girl* (ITV2).

Recording credits include: *Simply Heavenly* soundtrack, *Return of the Jedi*, Toni Morrison's *Beloved*.

Allyson also won the MOBO Award for Best Unsigned Act in 1998

Jennifer Saayeng
Ree

Theatre credits include: *City of Angels* (Donmar Warehouse), *A Long and Happy Life* (Finborough Theatre), *The Color Purple* (Menier Chocolate Factory), *X Factor the Musical, The Praise Singer* (Workshop), *Ghost* (Piccadilly), *Chess* (Toronto), *Hairspray* (original UK tour), *Not Quite Gospel* (Custard Factory), *Sister Act* (Kilworth House), *Zanna Don't!* (Landor).

Film credits include: *Prince of Persia.*

Television credits include: *Britannia High.*

Nina Toussaint-White
Tree

Theatre credits include: *Susan in Race* (Hampstead Theatre), *Lin in Cloud Nine* (Italia Conti Edinburgh Fringe Festival).

TV and film credits include: *Holby City*, *EastEnders*, *Doctor Who*, *Daughters*, *Casualty* (BBC), *Uncle* (Baby Cow/BBC3), *Death in Paradise* (Red Planet Productions), Series lead in *S*WITCH* (Touchpaper TV/ITV2), *Scott and Bailey* (Red Productions), *Whitechapel* (Carnival Film & Television), *The Fun Police* (Roughcut TV (ITV), *The Bill* (ITV).

Audio credits include: *Miss Selfridge Opening Store Radio* (Global/ Canvas), *Lonely Planet Audio Walking Tours* (Covent Garden), *A Thing inside a Thing inside a Thing* (BBC Radio) and *Take Me to Victoria Park* (BBC Radio).

Nikki Yeoh
On piano

As an internationally respected jazz musician Nikki has appeared alongside Roy Ayers, Neneh Cherry, Jean Carne, Chick Corea, Jools Holland, Eddie Harris, Dick Heckstall-Smith, Nigel Kennedy, Alexander O' Neil, Courtney Pine, John Surman, Cleveland Watkiss, Steve Williamson. She has collborated with the fiercely original hip-hop group The Roots and American R'n'B legends the Crown Heights Affair.

Accomplished soloist as she is, Nikki Yeoh has also excelled as a composer over the years and this is borne out by the number of very significant commissions she has to her name. Among the most notable recent works is a piece for the internationally renowned reeds virtuoso, John Surman, which premiered at the 2010 Cheltenham International Jazz Festival. Prior to that, in 2006, Yeoh presented River Spirit, which was written for the choir of New College, Oxford, following a commission from Oxford Contemporary Music. She was commissioned by piano circus to write *Six as One*, a series of short pieces for six pianos. She wrote *Entwined* and *Flora and Fauna* for piano virtuoso Joanna MacGregor. Nikki's new album *Solo Gemini* will be released in 2016

Theatre and film work includes: *Wheel Man*, directed by Benji Reid, *Speechmik X-ploration* for Bath Festival.

Creative Team Biographies

Ché Walker
Writer and Director

Ché trained at the Webber Douglas Academy of Dramatic Art.

Theatre writing credits include: *The Lightning Child* (Shakespeare's Globe Theatre), *The 8th* (Manchester International Festival 2011, Barbican Centre, Latitude and national tour 2012), *Lovesong* (Pleasance Dome, Crucible Sheffield, Manchester Royal Exchange, Albany Empire 2010), *Been So Long The Musical* (Young Vic – Winner Music Matters Judge's Award, nominated Evening Standard Best Musical, What's on Stage Best New Musical), *The Frontline* (Shakespeare's Globe Theatre), *Crazy Love* (Paines Plough).

Theatre directing credits include: *His Greatness* (Finborough Theatre), *Fog* (Finborough Theatre, Park Theatre and National Tour 2013), *Danny and the Deep Blue Sea* (Southwark Playhouse), *Blue Surge* (Finborough Theatre), *Little Baby Jesus* (Oval House), *Zelda* (Charing Cross Hotel), *Estate Walls* (Oval House), *Been So Long The Musical* (Young Vic, English Touring Theatre).

Acting credits include: *Youngers* (E4), *Holby City*, *EastEnders* (BBC1), *Judge John Deed*, *The Office* (Stephen Merchant/Ricky Gervais), *January 2nd* (Matt Winn), *Bedlam* (Vadim Jean), *Circus* (Rob Walker), *Kiss Kiss Bang Bang* (Stuart Suggs), *Tuesday* (Edward Bond), *Tuesday Night Poker* (Theatre Row, 42nd St), *New York* (Ray Virgo), *Othello* (Shakespeare's Globe), *Love's Labour's Lost* (Shakespeare's Globe/ National Theatre of Korea).

Annoushka Lucas
Songs and Musical Supervisor

Anoushka studied Russian and Italian at Oxford University.

Theatre credits include: *Klook's Last Stand* (Park Theatre), *The Ballad of L'il Benny – workshop* (Bush Theatre) *and Scorched Earth – workshop* (Independent).

Separately to her theatre work, Anoushka is a jazz singer and songwriter. In 2013 she won the Jazz FM Love Supreme Competition. She is currently working on an album with her quartet, ALQ, to be released in autumn 2015.

Sheila Atim
Additional songs

Sheila Trained at the Wac Arts. *The Etienne Sisters* is Sheila's songwriting and composition debut for theatre.

Theatre credits include: *Volpone*, *The Jew of Malta*, *Love's Sacrifice* (RSC Swan Season 2015), *Klook's Last* Stand by Ché Walker (Park Theatre), *Hopelessly Devoted* by Kate Tempest (Paines Plough), *Rachel* by Angelina Weld Grimke (Finborough Theatre), *Ghost Town* by Jessica Fisher (Pilot Theatre), *The Lightning Child* by Ché Walker (Shakespeare's Globe).

Sheila also writes music as a solo artist and has performed in various London venues, including indig02 and the Bush Theatre.

Ti Green
Set and Costume Designer

Ti studied English Literature at Cambridge University and Theatre Design at the Slade School of Art.

Theatre credits include: *Richard III*, *Little Eagles*, *Coriolanus* (RSC tour/Old Vic), *Julius Caesar* (RSC tour/Lyric Hammersmith), *Revenger's Tragedy*, *The Five Wives of Maurice Pinder*, *The UN Inspector* (National Theatre), *Coram Boy* (National Theatre, Imperial Theatre, New York), *I Am Not Myself These Days*, *The Spalding Suite* (*Fuel Theatre*), *The Fun Fair*, *Romeo and Juliet* (Home, Manchester), *Playing for Time* (Sheffield Crucible), *Bright Phoenix* (Liverpool Everyman), *The Snow Queen* (Nuffield), *A Woman in Mind* (Dundee and Birminingham Rep), *Orlando* (Manchester Royal Exchange), *A Christmas Carol* (Birmingham Rep), *Henry VI Parts I*, *II and III* (Globe), *A Midsummer Night's Dream* (Theatre Royal Northampton), *Time and the Conways* (Edinburgh Lyceum and Dundee Rep), *Unleashed* (Barbican), *The Resistible Rise of Arturo Ui* (Liverpool Playhouse and Nottingham Playhouse).

Ti's nominations and awards include two Tony Award nominations and an Outer Critics Circle Award nomination, for *Coram Boy* (Imperial Theatre, NY), a TMA nomination for *Paradise Lost* (Bristol Old Vic), an Evening Standard nomination for *The Revenger's Tragedy* (National Theatre) and a Manchester Theatre Award for *Romeo and Juliet* (Home, Manchester).   www.tigreen.net

Patience James
Choreographer

Patience James is a dancer, choreographer, actress, singer and all-round creative being who has graced many prestigious platforms with her explosive energy.

Patience trained on Wac Arts' three-year professional musical theatre course and East London Dance.

She is also a co-founder and dancer of her own dance duo (GOP Dancers) who will be performing this year at *Dance Afrique* at the Wembley arena.

Theatre credit include: *Oliva Tweest* (Hackney Empire), *Concrete Jungle* (Peacock Theatre/Edinburgh Fringe), *Ah Men!* (Soho Theatre), *Black and Blue Reading* (Tricycle Theatre), *Journeys Beyond* (Arcola Tent/Edinburgh Fringe), *Breakin' Convention* (Sadler's Wells) and *Twelve* (Birmingham Mac), Rich Mix, (Watermans).

Dance platforms include: O2 arena/indigo, Brixton Academy, Wembley Arena, Sadler's Wells, and *The X Factor* for many artists, including David Guetta, Emeli Sande', Cher Lloyd and Fuse Odg.

Arnim Friess
Lighting Designer

Arnim trained and worked as a photographer and audio-visual media designer in his native Germany, before moving to the UK to study scenography, receiving an MA at Birmingham Institute of Art and Design. He is the founder member of Pixelbox Ltd, which specialises in designing dynamic performance environments, blending lighting, motion graphics and video projection, animation and film-making. His lighting and projection designs have been seen not only in theatres around the world, but also in a zoo, a monastery, an abandoned pub and deep down in a cave.

Recent designs include: *Best Man* (Everyman Cork), *Alice in Wonderland* (Polka Theatre), *Shhh* (C12 Dance Theatre), *Leviathan* (Matadero Madrid), *Stars in the Morning Sky, For Talking Birds, We love you City, Too Much Pressure, One Night in November, The Dark Side of Buffoon, Monged* (with Fishambles, Dublin), *Puntila and His Man Matti, The Mysteries, Rumpelstiltskin* (Belgrade Theatre), *Piaf, Entertaining Mr Sloan, Hello Dolly, Gypsy* and *42nd Street* (Curve Leicester), *Ghosts in the Walls* (Royal Shakespare Company), *Grandpa in My Pocket* (Nottingham Playhouse and touring), *The Awkward Squad* (Arts Theatre, West End), *Gulliver's Travels* (Dragonbreath Theatre), *The Rememberers* (Birmingham REP with Apples&Snakes), *Space Odyssey* (Orchestra of the Swan), *Forever in Your Debt* (Foursight Theatre), *The Suicide, An Inspector Calls* (Theatr Clwyd), *Wander* (Hong Kong) and *Take* (Washington D.C.), *Lucky Seven* (Hampstead Theatre), *The Death of Harry Leon* (Ouroborus Theatre Dublin), National Holocaust Memorial Day in Coventry (Blue Eyed Soul Dance Company).

Louis Price
Video Designer

Louis graduated from Central St Martin's School of Art. He is a director, editor and producer of films and documentaries. He also designs and creates video imagery for theatre, dance and opera productions.   www.louisprice.co.uk

Recent designs include: *Orango* (BBC Proms/Royal Festival Hall/Helsinki Festival/Baltic Sea Festival Stockholm), *The Funfair* (Home, Manchester), *L'Enfant et les Sortileges* (Royal Festival Hall/Philarmonia Orchestra), *Five Soldiers – The Body is the Frontline* (Birmingham Rep, UK tour), *Bright Phoenix* (Liverpool Everyman), *Unleashed* (Barbican Theatre), *Sluts of Possession* (Edinburgh Festival/Film Fabriek Belgium), *There Is Hope* (UK tour), *Amphytrion* (Schauspielhaus Graz), *Wings of Desire* (Circa/International Dance Festival Birmingham), *The Resistible Rise of Arturo Ui* (Liverpool Playhouse), *The Ballad of the Sad Café R&D* (Moulins des Paillard, France), *Beside the Sea* (WOW Festival, Purcell Room, Southbank Centre).

Louis also curated the film elements of the *Patrice Chereau tribute* at the Young Vic. He is is a director of November Films (www.novemberfilms.co.uk), an independent film production and distribution company. For November Films he has directed the documentary *Beyond Biba – A Portrait of Barbara Hulanicki* (SkyArts/Sundance Channel), and is in development with *Exegesis – A Very British Cult* (BBC Wonderland/November Films).

Other recent film work includes: as editor, *Best* (Sundance Film Festival 2014), *In Mid Wickedness* (Tbilisi International Film Festival). As Director of Photography, *Five Soldiers Installation* (Herbert Gallery, Coventry/Stadtmuseum, Dresden), and as director, *Alexander DaCunha – Mix* (Thomas Dance Gallery, London), John Davies – *I Call Myself a Haunted House* (Marlborough Fine Art, London).

Sarah Weltman

Sound Designer

For Theatre Royal Stratford East: *Crowning Glory*.

Other sound design credits include: *The Full Monty* (UK Tour), *The Life and Times of Fanny Hill*, *Swallows and Amazons*, *Wild Oats* (Bristol Old Vic), *Ring Cycle Cyclotrope*, *De-loiite Ignite* (Royal Opera House), *Downstairs Four Minutes Twelve Seconds*, *The Empty Quarter*, *Donny's Brain* (Hampstead Theatre), *Wedding* (Shoreditch Town Hall), *Next Thing You Know*, *A Winter's Tale*, *The Hired Man* (Landor Theatre), *Benvenuto Cellini* (English National Opera), *Caligula*, *The Damnation of Faust*, *Idomeneo* (Synergy Theatre Project), *Girls Like That* (Unicorn Theatre) *Den of Thieves*, *Cape*, *Burning Bird*, *Glengarry Glen Ross*, *Convictions New Plays Festival* (Soho Theatre), *The Riots* (Tricycle Theatre).

Associate sound designer credits include: *Jeeves and Wooster*, *Perfect Nonsense*, *The Full Monty* (original tour and West End), *Inside Wagner's Head* (Plymouth Theatre Royal), *Street Scene* (Young Vic), *Swallows and Amazons* (Vaudeville Theatre and UK tour), *One Flew over the Cuckoo's Nest* (Garrick Theatre and UK tour).

Sound Designer and Consultant: Sam Wanamaker Playhouse at Shakespeare's Globe Theatre, the Globe to Globe Season 2012 and York University Theatre, Film and Television facility built in 2011.

Will Burton for David Grindrod Associates
Casting Director

Will has worked with David Grindrod and Stephen Crockett at David Grindrod Associates since 2007. Most recently Will was the casting director for the critically acclaimed transfer production of *In The Heights*, the ensemble company of *High Society* at the Old Vic, *Bugsy Malone* at the Lyric Hammersmith and for the European premiere of Harvey Fierstein's play, *Casa Valentina*.

DGA West End casting includes: *CATS, Made In Dagenham, Urinetown, The Commitments, Matilda, Once, Mamma Mia!, Shrek, Sweeney Todd* (English National Opera), *Ghost, Sister Act, Hairspray & A Chorus Line.*

Touring and regional casting includes: *The Smallest Show on Earth* (tour), *Monty Python Live* (O2 Arena), *Jesus Christ Superstar* (World Arena tour), *Oliver!, My Fair Lady* (Sheffield Crucible), *Fings Ain't What They Used to Be* (Theatre Royal, Stratford), *Paper Dolls* (Tricycle), *Carnival of Animals* (Riverside Studios).

Film credits include: Musical casting: *Beauty and the Beast* (Disney), directed by Bill Condon; UK Dancer casting: *Nine*, directed by Rob Marshall; and ensemble casting: *Mamma Mia!*, directed by Phyllida Lloyd and *The Phantom of the Opera*, directed by Joel Schumacher.

Television credits include: *The Voice, I'd Do Anything, Any Dream Will Do, How to Solve a Problem Like Maria* (BBC), *Superstar* (ITV) and *Over the Rainbow* (TalkbackThames).

Will is a full member of the Casting Directors' Guild of Great Britain.

Greta Gould
Assistant Director

Greta trained as an actress at Drama Studio London.

Assistant directing credits include: *Klook's Last Stand* (Park Theatre), *Iphigeneia at Aulis* (Wac Arts), *Hammer Ring*, reading (Map Studio Café).

Acting credits include: *Henry V* (Union Theatre), *A Doll's House* (The Space), Fragments of a Fallen City (*Regency Tavern, Brighton*), *A Neon Fairytale* (Roundhouse, Contact Theatre, Manchester), *Your Number's Up* (Roundhouse, Assembly Rooms, Edinburgh), *Tiger Country* (New Diorama Theatre).

Greta is also co-founder and director of Equilibrium Promotions Ltd, whose aim is to connect industry professionals and showcase developing writers, as well as directors and actors. We are particularly interested in supporting work that provides significant opportunities for women and professionals of minority ethnic backgrounds. Our regular event *One Hour* gives producers, theatre and film makers a unique opportunity to see selected new dramatic works at Soho Theatre.

Theatre Royal Stratford East Staff

ADMINISTRATION AND OPERATIONS

Darren Spencer
Building Maintenance Technician

Graeme Bright
Building and Facilities Manager/DPS

Lee Henderson
General Manager

Leighton Lewis
Bar and Catering Manager

Mary Caws
Executive Director

Stuart Saunders
IT Systems Manager

Velma Fontaine
Operations Coordinator

ARCHIVES

Mary Ling
Assistant Archivist

Murray Melvin
Theatre Archivist

ARTISTIC

Fadi Tavoukdjian
Musical Theatre New Writing Manager

Karen Fisher
Associate Producer

Kerry Michael
Artistic Director

Pooja Ghai
Resident Director

Rita Mishra
Assistant to Artistic Director

ARTISTIC ASSOCIATES

Fred Carl (US)
John Gordon **Team Angelica**
Matthew Xia
Rikki Beadle-Blair **Team Angelica**
Robert Lee (US)
ULTZ

BAR AND KITCHEN STAFF

Azuka Essu-Taylor, Hannah Pharaoh
(Team Leader), Kellie Murphy, Luke
Simpson, Matt pearson, Marcin
Zawistowski **(Bar Duty Manager)**,
Maya Essu-Taylor, Nathan Dixon, Peter
Rodriguez, Pravie Maharaj **(Shift leader)**
and Unique Spencer **(Team Leader)**,
Christian Johnson **(Head Chef)**, Cynthia
Adumoah, Laurie Ann Anderson, Leonard
Headlam, Lois-Ann Messiah, Rayshawn
Charles and Sydney Weise.

BOX OFFICE

Amaryllis Courtney, Angela Frost
(Box Office Manager), Asha Bhatti,
Beryl Warner **(Box Office Supervisor)**,
Eyesha Mingo, Julie Lee.

DEVELOPMENT

Chris Alexander
Development Officer

Fiona Joseph
Development Administrator

Sally Goldsmith
**Director of Development and
Communications**

DOMESTIC ASSISTANTS

Manjit Kaur Babbra and Marjorie Walcott

FINANCE

Andrew Voronin
Head of Finance (Interim)

Sibhatlab Kesete
Finance Officer

Titilayo Onanuga
Finance Officer

Our vision is unlimited but our funding is not . . .

The support of individuals, business partners and charitable trusts is essential in creating our world-class programme.

The Etienne Sisters would not have been possible without the generous support of our funders, and we invite you to join us to ensure future productions find their home on our historic stage.

We are proud that we change lives with performances and projects that are both relevant to our community and reach an international audience.

Supporting this vital work has never been easier: you can join our Vision Collective members, become a Business Partner, name a seat, or make a one-off donation. Your support will ensure the continuation of our work on stage, as well as our inspirational programme for young people and our community.

For more information or a chat, please contact Sal Goldsmith, Development Director, on 020 8279 1176 or email sgoldsmith@stratfordeast.com.

We would like to thank the following for their support

Major Donors

Scrutton Estates Ltd,
The Sahara Care Charitable Trust

Vision Collective

Pioneers Andrew Cowan, Angela & Stephen Jordan, Ed Ross, Elizabeth & Derek Joseph, Sabine Vinck, Trevor Williams and all those who wish to remain anonymous

Directors Collective Hedley G. Wright, Rachel Potts for Jon Potts, and all those who wish to remain anonymous

Business Supporters

Adnams
ArcelorMittal
Attic Storage and Removals Solutions
Bloomberg
Devonshires Solicitors
English Cities Fund
Galliard Homes
Hotel Novotel London Excel
Lend Lease
Morgan Sindall
Telford Homes Plc

Trusts and Fundationss

The Andrew Lloyd Webber Foundation
Calouste Gulbenkian Foundation
Clifford Chance Foundation
Esmée Fairbairn Foundation
Garfield Weston Foundation
The Gibbs Charitable Trust
The Mackintosh Foundation
Newham Giving Fund
Paul Hamlyn Foundation
The Theatres Trust
The Wolfson Foundation

We would like to acknowledge the generous support of The Monument Trust.

We also would like to express our thanks to Frantic Assembly, London Borough of Newham for *Every Child A Theatregoer* and Plashet School.

...a people's theatre

Theatre Royal Stratford East is a prolific developer of new work, attracting artists and audiences often not represented in many other venues. This award-winning theatre, located in the heart of London's East End on the edge of the new Queen Elizabeth Olympic Park, prides itself on creating world class work that reflects the concerns, hopes and dreams of its community. Through a continuous loop it inspires and is inspired by its vibrant, young and diverse audience.

Contacting Theatre Royal Stratford East:

Theatre Royal Stratford East
Gerry Raffles Square
Stratford, London
E15 1BN

www.stratfordeast.com / theatreroyal@stratfordeast.com

 theatreroyalstratfordeast

 @stratfordeast

Box Office & Information
020 8534 0310
Mon–Sat, 10am–6pm

Typetalk
07972 918 050

Fax
020 8534 8381

Administration Line
020 8534 7374

The Etienne Sisters

Ché Walker studied acting at the Webber Douglas
Academy in London. His first play, *Been So Long*,
premiered at the Royal Court Theatre in 1998, was
runner-up for both the Meyer-Whitworth and the John
Whiting Awards and has been performed in Sweden,
Denmark, Germany, New Zealand and Australia. *Flesh
Wound* premiered at the Royal Court in 2003 and won
the George Devine Award for Most Promising Playwright.
The Frontline, with music by Arthur Darvill, was written
whilst he was appearing at Shakespeare's Globe in 2008,
and was the first play with a contemporary setting to be
staged at the Globe. Other plays include *Crazy Love*
(Paines Plough/Òran Mór, 2007), *Been So Long the
Musical* (Young Vic, 2009), *Lovesong* (English Touring
Theatre, 2010), *The 8th*, with Paul Heaton (Manchester
International Festival, 2011/national tour, 2012), *The
Lightning Child* (the first musical to be performed at
Shakespeare's Globe, 2013) and *Klook's Last Stand* (Park
Theatre, 2014). Ché has directed over twenty professional
theatre productions, and teaches acting technique at
RADA, Stella Adler Academy Los Angeles and Wac Arts.
He has taught writing for the Royal Court Young Writers'
Programme, in the Feltham Young Offenders' Institute,
at the Centrepoint Homeless Shelter and for Hampstead
Theatre Youth Project.

by the same author

BEEN SO LONG
THE FRONTLINE
FLESH WOUND

CHÉ WALKER

The Etienne Sisters

FABER & FABER

First published in 2015
by Faber and Faber Ltd
74–77 Great Russell Street
London WC1B 3DA

Typeset by Country Setting, Kingsdown, Kent CT14 8ES
Printed in England by CPI Group (UK) Ltd, Croydon CR0 4YY

A CIP record for this book
is available from the British Library

978-0-571-32924-3

2 4 6 8 10 9 7 5 3 1

Special Thanks

Kerry Michael, Dawn Reid, Pooja Ghai
and all at Theatre Royal Stratford East,
Sasha Frost, Greta Gould, Wreh-Asha Walton,
Amanda Wilkin, Gemma Knight Jones,
Celia Greenwood, Steve Medlin, Anthony Lennon,
Julian Cox, Ed Blunt, and all at Wac Arts
for their generosity in supporting
the development of *The Etienne Sisters*

The Etienne Sisters was first presented at the Theatre Royal, Stratford East, on 10 September 2015. The cast was as follows:

Bo Allyson Ava-Brown
Ree Jennifer Saayeng
Tree Nina Toussaint-White

Duvivier Anthony Lennon
Mother Jo Martin

On piano Nikki Yeoh

Written and directed by Ché Walker
Songs by Anoushka Lucas
Additional songs by Sheila Atim
Designer Ti Green
Musical Supervisor Anoushka Lucas
Musical Director Nikki Yeoh
Choreographer Patience James
Lighting Designer Arnim Friess
Video Designer Louis Price
Sound Designer Sarah Weltman
Casting Director Will Burton,
    for David Grindrod Casting
Singing Coach Rachel Bennett
Assistant Director Greta Gould

Characters

Tree

Ree

Bo

THE ETIENNE SISTERS

Bo
> As we face the setting sun
> And all is said and all is done
> I reminisce on battles lost

Tree
> Demons real and demons fake
> With fangs of pearl, ferocious snakes
> Chilled to the bone, an early frost

All Three
> And family ain't all it's cracked up to be
> And family is a trap to me
> And family ain't all it's cracked up to be
> And family is a trap to me

Ree
> Family is no place to be
> Sharp elbows, petty jealousies

All Three
> As we face the setting sun
> Reminisce on battles won
> What is done can never be undone
> And family ain't all it's cracked up to be
> Family, petty jealousies

Ree
> As we face the setting sun
> And all is said and all is done
> I reminisce on battles lost

Tree Our mother passed. Not a surprise 'cause she'd
been dying for a while, piece by piece and breath by

breath just disappearing from us. Kinda relieved when she gave up the fight and let the Lord take her. But still shitty. Obviously.

Our mother's last words – 'Oban'. Place up in Scotland. Right by the sea. Gets this soft light and fresh crab. Family holiday. Million a years back. Things went wrong there. Drama and cataclysm. Dunno why this is what she's thinking juss before she popping her clogs but there it is. One word.

'Oban'.

I had to sort out the funeral. Invites and that. Time off from that flipping checkout till. Boss gimme hard time, but when iss a funeral, ain't nuttin they can say. One person I most decidedly ain't inviting is my jellyfish half-sister called Bo.

Jellyfish never die. When they decompose, a coupla cells split free from the corpse and regenerate into another jellyfish. If you chop a jellyfish in half, it just becomes two jellyfish. Boy jellyfish don't even need girl jellyfish to reproduce. The jellyfish has increased it's numbers by ten times in recent years. Iss jellyfish thass gonna inherit this earth once we humans finally blow the planet into pieces. I'm telling you man, jellyfish all up in this thing. Thass why I call my half-sister Bo a jellyfish.

Impossible to get rid of. No brains, but deadly sting. Her name – Bo was short for summink. And you know what? I never knew what it was short for.

You had to remind y'self you had a half-sister, y'know? Like, no link, like . . .

Seemed natural that I didn't invite Bo. Whafor?

But, y'know all day I got this feeling in my water that I'm gonna see her.

And sure as eggs is eggs there she is by the graveside.

Wid da Bambi eyes and the simpering lips.

My back arch like puma in the savannah but this is me, lemme stay cool while we lay my Old Dear to rest.

She sings.

The deepest grief
Bereavement
Bereavement and hurt
The sweetest sleep
Deliverance
Deliverance from hurt
This life of hard toil
Released back into the soil
And souls ascend
To the Kingdom
A life ends
In freedom
The deepest grief
Bereavement
Bereavement and hurt
The sweetest sleep
Deliverance
Deliverance from hurt
Nothing ever ends
No one ever dies
So make amends
As you look into God's eyes
The deepest grief
Bereavement
Bereavement and pain
The sweetest sleep
Deliverance
Deliverance from pain
A life of sacrifice
Our memories they must suffice
Souls are soaring on the wing
So lift your voice in prayer and sing

Now back with the swept-clean house and the cousins
you ain't never heard of all of us sweating in black and

the jellyfish does what I know she's gonna do, direct beam straight for my sister, my full-sister but – what-a-burden-to-carry – Ree, I knew she was gonna target my Ree and I knew she was gonna reel her in and thus my own shtuppid self and this is how the damn sordid charade did unfurl.

Ree Wow.

Bo I know.

Ree Whassit been?

Bo Hard to count.

Ree Five years?

Bo 'Bout five years, yeah.

Ree Five years . . .

Bo Yeah.

Ree So where you been?

Bo Condolences, Ree. On the real. Such a elegant woman. Always carried h'self juss nice. Presentable, y'kna ? At all times.

Ree Yeah, she looked good.

Bo Thass one woman knew how to wear a hat.

Ree So where you been five years?

Bo She could buss a chapeau.

Ree She most certainly could rock a bonnet iss true.

Bo And lovely to me oh my gosh.

Ree Aahh.

Bo Couldna asked for a better stepmum in truth.

Ree Oh thass nice of you to say . . .

Bo Lovely to me.

Ree 'Cause iss –

Bo Lovely to me at all times.

Ree A strange situation –

Bo So welcoming when I come round to the house.

Ree You being, uh, not from –

Bo 'Member Oban? What was we, like ten or eleven?

Ree Oban, oh gosh.

Bo She juss welcomed me into the fold and we both know she didn't have to and we both know most women woulda said, 'What?! Get this child away from me' – but not your mum oh no juss graceful and kind and I never forget the light up there and the sea and the briny smell and truth be told thass a precious memory for me, like, precious 'cause iss the last time things was simple and I dunno like a purity to it, y'know?

Ree Yeah, Oban was jokes . . . That light up there!

Bo She was kind to me at a time when I needed kindness you know? What with my mum and that.

Ree How is your mum? Is she still, uh –

Bo And to this day I wear this that she gimme –

Bo shows Ree a necklace round her neck.

Ree I remember that necklace.

Bo Nice, innit.

Ree You sayin she gave you that?

Bo And even though iss obviously a mad sorrowful occasion, I like feel happy . . . most probly coming over like a crazy person but . . . well, she ain't suffering no

19

more, y'kna? And we celebrate that. And we celebrate her life. Her, whassit, accomplishments.

Ree Oh I dunno . . . Hers was a little life.

Bo Nah man. Her life was monumental. Look at you. How she raised you. What an achievement. You are a daughter to be proud of, and a sister to, to, to, just squeeze up.

Ree Oh.

Bo For real.

Ree Thass nice.

Bo Yeah.

Ree Yeah.

Bo I know I been on my sojourn, sis. I mean, what, half a decade since last we squeezed? And most prob'ly five years before that too. Found myself in some hard hard corners, I been tested to my frickin soul, truss –
    And we both know I always kinda liked the shadow-world a little too much . . .

Done some things I never thought I'd do. Survival, like . . .

But one lesson been lessoned . . . is that Family is Sanctuary.

And thass why I come down here, Ree. To support.

Ree Thank you, sis.

Bo And I'm gonna stay here for a while. In the house, like.

Ree Oh, uh –

Bo Seriously. I wanna do it and I'm happy to do it. I'm gonna stay and juss . . . whatever it takes, y'know?

Ree Uh . . . Thank you . . .

Bo And, you know . . . I'll stay as long as it takes for you to get back on your feet. It's no problem! We're family, not so?

Pause.

We're family, not so?

Ree Course. But y'know what, Bo, I –

Bo So what, shall I take Mum's room?

Ree NO!

Bo No?

Ree Juss . . . juss not Mum's room, OK?

Bo Well, I ain't doing the couch.

Ree We can share.

Bo Share?

Ree Share my room.

Bo You take the couch.

Ree Me.

Bo And I'll take your room.

Ree My room.

Bo If you don't want me around then I can always –

Ree I didn't mean to come across like that . . .

Bo Come across like what?

Ree Course you can take my room.

Bo Sure?

Ree Positive.

Bo Cause y'know that was a bit hurtful.

Ree Oh Bo . . .

Bo Nuffink an apology wouldn't put right.

Ree I'm sorry.

Bo Do you love me?

Ree Y'know it.

Bo I don't always know it, sis.

Ree I love you.

Bo I love you too.

   Tree comes in.

Tree Hm.

Bo Tree! How yuh doing sis?

Tree I juss buried my mum.

   Pause.

Bo Iss good to see yuh.

   Pause.

Ree Sis . . . Bo is gonna stay with us for a while.

Tree Can I have a word widjou please? A word with you alone. Like in private, yeah?

Bo I'like how you're doing your hair.

Tree OK.

Bo Very bold.

Tree Ree. A word. Now.

Bo What?

Tree What?

Bo What?

Ree Bo, wouldjuh mind juss . . . only for a minute.

Bo Only for a minute what?

Tree (*gritted teeth*) Get this girl outta here . . .

Ree Juss like step outside for a bit like.

Bo Outside?

Ree For a bit.

Bo Kinda chilly still.

Tree Seriously, I'm about to –

Bo What was that, Tree? Can't hear whatchour sayin.

Ree Just for a minute, yeah? Juss for a minute.

Bo is about to exit.

Bo Yeah. Hair looks good.

She exits.

Tree I am pissed off officially. That girl is a pagan to my eyes.

Ree Iss our mum's funeral, Tree. I can't take some sorta Warrior Cry right at this moment. Please. Vulnerable, yeah?

Tree Why she wanna stay?

Ree Support us.

Tree Nonsense.

Ree Iss not.

Tree Iss nonsense, sis.

Ree C'mon.

Tree After summmink.

Ree She's not.

Tree After summmink I can tell.

Ree Tree –

Tree She blows into town like once in a blue moon and whips up some madness then duss out, here's me picking up the pieces.

Ree Let her try.

Tree Try what, though? Born thief.

Ree The past ain't too delicious, thass true, but she is blood to us.

Tree Genetics ain't the same as *love*.

Ree I need her.

Tree No, you don't need her, you need me.

Ree Juss let her stay, thass all.

Tree Ree . . .

Ree Let her stay.

Tree I'm juss watchin out for you, y'know.

Ree I know.

Tree Your decision-making ain't always the best, is it? You'd be the first to admit that.

Ree You done well today.

Tree Yeah?

Ree Service and that.

Tree Think so?

Ree Yeah man. Mum would have been very –

Tree Alright, alright, alright.

Ree Only thing that woulda been better –

Tree Don't.

Ree Was if you'd –

Tree Don't say it.

Ree Y'know how she loved to hear you play that –

Tree I don't do that no more.

Ree Y'sounded so good back then.

Tree And y'know why I don't play. Causa the Jellyfish.

Awkward silence.

Ree That big belly man who reckons he's some kinda uncle to us has let off two of the most noxious mustard gas farts I have ever smelt in my whole entire life.

Despite herself, Tree laughs.

We got some weird cousins, boy!

Tree Innit though! Woman all weeping and wailing and I don't think she spent more than one hour with our mum. Coming like she gonna fling herself in the grave with her.

Ree 'Magine Mum! 'Ah, who the arse is this woman? I don't know you!'

Tree 'Come out my coffin!'

Ree Innit

Tree Who are they?

Ree Lunatics.

Tree And the wall-eyed fella with the giant wart on his neck –

Ree We can't be related.

Tree We are, y'know.

Ree We're doomed! Ha!

Tree Iss juss us, you know that, Ree? Juss you and me.

Ree Juss give her a chance.

Bo re-enters.

Bo Can I come in? The livin flatulence up in that room.

Tree Whassat necklace round your neck?

Bo covers the necklace.

Is that what I think it is?

Ree Tree, juss . . . uh? Iss such a day of pain.

Bo Boy! Elephant tusk in the room so less exorcise some shit so we can juss be clean and free and get to loveliness, yeah, Tree? Steada cutting your eye and twissing up yuh lip every time your eye set upon me.

I been away and now I'm back so you muss juss deal widdat.

I know you dislike me, and there's nothing I can do about until you're ready.

Tree Until *I'm* –?

Bo The more time you spend wimme, the more you'll see that I made a big change.

Tree Ha!

Bo Used to this crap from you and all them people who don't wanna acknowledge what I been through and where I'm at now. Caterpillar to butterfly bussing out dat chrysalis and you gotta see that.

    I'll tell you what I told our sister –

Tree *My* sister –

Bo I'm here for the two a' you, understand? To support you whatever way I can.

Tree So whass the angle you anglin'?

Bo Whatchou say?

Tree Workin summink, I can tell. Tryna work some dark arts on this little one here –

Ree I'm actually older than you, sis. . .

Tree Juss 'cause she ain't smart juss 'cause she's suggestible you think you can –

Bo Tree, I know you're upset and grieving and –

Tree You ain't got the right to know I'm upset –

Bo And I know there's all kindsa reasons –

Tree Good reasons –

Bo – why I ain't what you wanna be looking at right now but can't we juss let a bygone go by? I wanna –
    Well –
    Tree it ain't right to be at each other's throats like this.
    I always looked up to you and even if you blocking off them memories you and me catch nuff joke back in the day nuff joke and we make up some silly songs also when you used to play your –
    Ah, c'mon, sis.

She sings.

I never meant for war
I only come in peace

If you could tell me please what
We're fighting for?

Let's leave the past behind
Why do we have to hate
Girl just let down your guard
You're so angry

Let love be between us Tree
Let love be between us Tree
Let love be between us three

Sister I understand
Cos we had a rocky start
Extend an open hand and heart

Let love be between us Tree
Let love be between us Tree
Let love be between us three

Ree This is summink I want and I'm not nobody, Tree.
I'm not nobody. And I want this.

Tree softens a little.

Tree Ok, Bo . . . I'm a-give you the benefit of a sizable
and substantial doubt. But I'm watching you X-ray vision
and ting.
   I'm watching you right through to the soul. Y'smell me?

Ree Bo is gonna be an asset to this family. Right, Bo?

Bo Thass what I'm wanting.

Tree Hhhmmm.

Ree I guarantee family harmony.
   (*To audience.*) Mad thing was, it worked! For a while.
Tree kinda bit her tongue and juss cool for a while, and
Bo . . . Bo wasn't carrying on like some many-headed sea
beast. Even . . . Well, take a look for y'selves.

Tree Ah God, I can't hold this thing up no more.

Bo Whatchou say?

Tree Oh! Thought I was on my J's.

Bo What can't you hold up?

Tree How long you been sitting all silent?

Bo What can't you hold up?

Tree Nothing.

Bo Go on.

Tree Juss caught me at a –

Bo Low ebb?

Tree Yeah.

Bo Whassit, work getting you down?

Tree This guy today yeah tryna tell me summink 'bout
he likes the way I look all heavy on the crotch in his eyes
and I tell him lissen yeah I'm not here for that I'm here to
scan your items and tot it all up for you and then help
you put it in a bag and if I was about fluttering my
eyelashes and simpering atchou then I'd let you know
and he's sticking out his tongue and flicking it at me.

Bo Hate when they do that.

Tree So I'm climbing out my till looking for my manager
to get some protection from this harassment but my
guv'nor waddles up and starts humiliating me in fronta
this fool and then –

Bo Go on.

Tree Then he has me tot him up and pack his bags for
him and just as a little cherry on top I gotta carry it out
to his car and I ain't meanta do that! I'm on the
checkout. Carrying shit out to the cars is the work they
give to the –

Bo Defectives.

Tree And this fool still tryna tell me what he wants to do to me, and the guv'nor had me carrying them heavy heavy sacks with all the take, all the pound coins and some paper too, I gotta take it up to the stinkin back office and put it in the safe for them aaargh –
    And money talks, y'know.
    Not like they say.
    It actually talks.
    Says all kinda rude shit.
    Especially the pound coins they're feisty.
    Telling me what you doing working for these guys ain't you got no oomph to you? Whass happened to your dreams?
    Shove 'em in the safe and lock 'em up and they're still cussing through the steel at me and there's me thinking can I afford to juss long off this job but since Mum – ahh – since Mum –

Bo S'okay, Tree.

Tree Sorry.

Bo I know.

Tree Y'never know when iss gonna hit.

Since Mum passed iss all on me and I ain't got no one to –

Bo I know.

Tree Turn to and that.

Bo Yeah.

Tree And Ree, well –

Bo She's the one turning to you.

Tree Exackly! Like I'm now the –

Bo Lissen.

Tree And I ain't always like –

Bo No one is.

Tree Agh.

Bo C'mon, sis. Whass happened to all that music you was making?

Tree Eh?

Bo Thass my memory of you. Up in Oban. You and me making up lyrics to songs and youse always plonking out summink and scraping that fiddle under your chin.

Tree Don't wanna bring that up. After you – Well, Oban . . . Mum went . . . and I swore I'd never –

Bo Thass a big part a' you though.

Tree Nuttin more than a phantom limb.

Bo Why not dust it all off?

Tree Come on . . .

Bo You used to sound nice, Tree. Like . . . nice, like. What you was playing. Nice. Make yuh sad, then make you kinda smile, all kindsa things . . .

Tree Really?

Bo You kidding? Beautiful stuff.

Tree My mum never thought so . . .

Bo What?

Tree Nah. No substance, she reckoned.

Bo I don't believe she would ever . . .

Tree Oh yeah. Bo . . . My mum ain't never said one good thing 'bout that violin thing, not once.

Once a person pass on iss like they become untouchable, like beyond reproach, but . . . Mum, well . . . sometimes she could juss . . .

Boom . . .

Some things you just can't talk to your sister about.

Bo But you can talk to me.

Tree . . . Yeah . . .

Bo Yeah.

Tree Had ways of putting you down you could feel the knife sliding in and then you question y'self like is this real what she's saying or am I dreaming the whole thing but then lying there and yeah she did say that about me and yeah it was dark and . . . and . . .

Bo I know.

Tree Jesus, I dunno where that come from. Whoo . . .

Bo C'm here.

Tree Easy.

Bo OK.

I'm juss relieved to hear your mum wasn't faultless. Always coming like Wonder Woman to my eyes. Dream Mother, you know? Role-model type fing. I gotta admit nuff times my jealousy burning hard, sis. Burning hard inside me. With my own mum and her troubles. Mum was like a homeless, sometimes, man! One step up from a homeless. Wild-ass woman.

Tree You never told me none a' that.

Bo Whole heap a' things we ain't never told each other.

Tree True.

Bo Whass the issue with the music?

Tree Phaaw.

Bo Whass holding you back?

Tree I'm juss a checkout girl.

Bo Nonsensical statement, sis.

Tree Three more years on the checkout and I can do the manager exam and thass dough, y'know? I can tough that out. My shoulders broad for a reason. Manager, then regional manager then mortgage and I can move out this stinking night of the living dead area . . .

Bo That you talking or your mum talking? Uh?

Tree Put them thing aside and put your shoulder to the wheel.

Bo Here's you thinking your talent belongs to you but it don't, Tree. Your talent belonging to the world.

Tree I ain't the *X Factor* type, si – uh, Bo.

Bo You gonna be burning up if you don't give it a go. Regret come lick you in your head, sis.

    Pause.

You like me more than you wanna, innit?

Tree Don't spoil it.

Bo Ha!

Tree Stop dat.

Bo Still ticklish?

Tree Don't even –

Bo You like me.

Tree Maybe . . .

Bo You like me.

Ree My sister Tree painted me as this vulnerable little bimbo that Bo could juss fill up and influence to the wrong. And that juss ain't who I am, y' know? I'm not weak. I'm not dumb. I can debate and politic, what?

Tree appointed herself as my protector. But I reckon this was a role she needed to believe she was.

Not what she actually was. 'Ah, Ree messed up again. Ah, Ree, such a weak-minded little girl what we gonna do?' Eff that! Eff off widdat!

My whole thing is I juss want everyone to get along and so don't make no fuss, bite your tongue and let belittlements slide, let petty tings juss wash off you for the sake of some convivial atmosphere, y'know?

But clouds ain't far from the horizon and next thing them same clouds 'bout to crap right on my head.

Ding dong on the door no one else in the crib . . .

Me on my J's opens it still in my dressing gown . . .

And when I say this man was big . . . The man block out the sun. Understand?

But that ain't whass scary 'bout him.

'Cause you knew . . . You juss knew . . .

From one look in them gunmetal grey slate eyes . . .

That this was a man who enjoyed taking lives.

Prayin he's got the wrong house but knowing that he's here for . . . He's here for . . .

He says:

'You Bo's sister?'

I nod my head and then it won't stop nodding.

'Where is she?'

My mouth opens and thass all it does.

Tell her Duvivier knocked for her.

Duvivier! The Duvivier?

I'd heard a' him but I thought he was a mythical creature.

Tell her Duvivier came for whass his.

Tell her I'll make her eat her own eyeballs with a spoon.

Tell her I'll cut her face off and replace with a goat's.
I will maim her so she can't speak or walk.
Understand?
I have no problem hurting women. Longest two
minutes of my life.
He turns away.
Me shaking sweating crying my fear making me into a
child.

Bo One time when I was little my mum gimme the dole
money and tells me get the shopping – she doesn't trust
herself so iss down to me so I go out and I spend the
whole thing on cookie dough ice cream and of course I
think this is gonna be fun and I eat until I puke
But.
This is whass different about me yeah.
Clean that puke off my chin rinse my mouth out and
yam off the next tub.
Ha!
This thing with Duvivier kinda like that too . . .
Duvivier and his murderous self ha! Can't help but take
the piss. Ever been driving and you think juss lemme turn
the wheel into oncoming traffic? Ever seen a policeman
gun and ya juss wanna grab it?
Here's what they don't tell ya. Social Workers.
Teachers. Psychiatric people, all them wankers.
When they tryna find out why you can't stop fighting
and robbing and drugging and kissing . . .
Here's the secret –
Iss FUN!

She sings.

Something 'bout being on the run

Something 'bout being on the run
God forgive me I think it's
Something 'bout the mad buzz
Something 'bout the mad buzz

35

Something 'bout knowing what I've done
Something 'bout knowing I'll outrun
The ones that chase me
Run the ones that chase me
The thrill, the tingle
Adrenalin
That's running through my veins
Running through my veins.

Verse 2: the same.

Chorus: the same.

Now I know I'm alive
My heart in overdrive
And I cannot believe there's more than this

Something 'bout being on the run

Times 4.

Ree Bo! What the heck . . .

Bo What?

Ree What you got y'self into?

Bo What?

Ree I had a visit from the Devil himself today.

Bo Oh.

Ree Summink you wanna tell me?

Bo Sis.

Ree Man talked to me like I was dirt!

Bo I never wanted you to get mixed up in all of it.

Ree Well, I'm mixed up! Mixed up to my knickers! THE
MAN IS HUGE! MURDEROUS! INSANE! So.

No flim-flam and no smoke and mirrors.

The truth.
The truth, Bo.

Bo So there's a little bit a' trouble I got myself into.

Ree Duvivier ain't little bit of trouble, Duvivier is Four Horseman on the Gallop.

Bo The way they're tellin it, they reckon I've rolled up to his house to buy myself a nice little bag a' thai stick, and that I'm sitting there billin' up and drinking a herb tea with Duvivier, juss nice, and Duvivier pops out the room to placate his missus, and this is what they say I done next, they say, yeah . . . that I, like out of nowhere, like, they say I jumped up and grabbed a big batch of cocaine and jumped out the window with it! Can you believe it, sis?

Ree Well . . .

Bo Eh? Me? I know. Like I'm capable of such lunacy.

Ree You *are* a bit wild, though, Bo . . .

Bo Outlandish in the extreme.

Ree Really?

Bo But the trouble is that they got in their heads and they won't budge, these people are a bit like capable of lavish violence, y'know?

Ree You did it, didncha? Truth on a Bible. You did it.

Bo I can't believe my own sister would say that.

Ree I can't believe my own sister would come with this thievery and anarchy to my door.

Bo They're making it up.

Ree Why would they make it up, Bo?

Bo I dunno . . .

Ree Why? What earthly reason would they have –?

Bo I can see you're panicking and stressing but lemme set your mind at ease and tell you there is absolutely zero chance of anyone actually popping off a hollow-point into any person's brain.

Well not zero chance but infinitesimal percentage, sis, y'know?

No one has any reason for no one to knock your door.

Ree No reason to knock my –? Well, what the frick was that creature on my doorstep then?

Bo I would never, ever, ever put you in the line of fire. You're my sister. Juss keep my head down and the curtains drawn and things blow over.

Ree Yuh can't stay here, Bo.

Bo Whatchou say to me?

Ree Aintchou got nowhere else to hide juhself?

Bo Maybe you don't see me as family . . .

Ree Bo, don't go on so.

Bo Nah, maybe we're getting down to the core a' this guestion, Ree . . . 'cause if you really saw me as family you wouldn't even prevaricate for a second.

Ree Thass not the case at all, Bo, and I don't think iss fair to be flinging them sorta statements around the place, you're more special to me than Special K and I love you more than I can express but this is some nefarious business you tryna entangle my arse up in . . . Bo, I am your sister and I'm scared and I – I –

She sings.

I been with you
Showed so much loyalty
Been true to you

Made myself all you see
But this is murder we talking
Cold-blooded murder you talking
And I don't know if I can follow you
Down this path of dread
And oh God if tomorrow
I hear somebody dead
I don't know if my mind will snap
Don't know if my heart will fail
One bad decision and major mishap
You sipping porridge in a London jail

This is madness you planning
All this scheming and scamming
Leads nowhere but disaster
Turn to tears, no more laughter
I seen the truth behind your swagger

You ain't no roughneck, put down your dagger
Throw madness in the river
You ain't a taker you're a giver
'Cause there's a look in your eyes
Belies a sweetness inside

And when your fingers entwine with mine
We take wing and we start to fly
You're acting bad but I know you're good

So set aside this path of blood
Vengeance is mine ain't no way to live
Vengeance is mine leaves no room to forgive
So join me in love
Heal me in love
Hold me in love.

Bo (*sings*)
    You didn't grow up like how I grew
    You see as lies what I know to be true
    And yes this road is a brutal path

And no man is free from his past
And if this thing don't get done quick-time
Iss me suffers, iss me dying
'Cause the simple math supposes
Me or him I never chose this
Just a victim of the circumstance
No I
Never had much of a chance
So I askin you to shelter me
Be strong for me, we're family
Sees me first, I'll be dropping
Scatter flowers in my coffin
You don't look so good all dressed in black, girl
Iss all about the fast react, girl
If you love me you would do it
Truly love me then you would do it
Say you love me and then do it

Tree (*to Bo*) If she loves you then she'd do what?

Ree Hey, Tree.

Tree If she loves you then she'd do what?

Bo This don't concern you.

Tree Everything to do with this one here concerns me.

Ree Sis, iss cool.

Tree No, it ain't cool!

Ree Iss juss she fallen foul of summink but we're sorting it out.

Tree She gonna be falling foul of my size tens up her jacksie in a minute.

Ree I'm on it, Tree. I'll think a' summink.

Tree What is this about? Serious enough not to tell me.

Ree Duvivier.

Tree WHAAAAT? How you mean –? Did you juss say Duvivier? *Duvivier* Duvivier? Duvivier the man who sets blowtorch to nipples on a daily? Duvivier the Demon? How could you say his name in the house our mother raised us in?

Right now she clawing her way out of her grave to slap you round the face for this! Shame on the family name! Am I the only one who listened to her teachings? All that praying and rocking and this is how you sully the woman's memory! Duvivier the Madman! Duvivier, oh my God! GET OUT! GET OUT GET OUT GET OUT!

Bo Calm y'self, flapping about ain't doing nuffink for my nerves.

Tree (*suddenly calm*) I'd appreciate it if you just left the house and caught a wasting disease and die real slow but far away from my sister and my house.

Bo Where am I supposed to go?

Tree Oh, I'll tell you where you can go –

Bo This ain't nutting to do wid this drama with Duvivier, this is juss years of resentment vomiting up outta you, innit? You been looking for a way to make me vanish since day.

Tree And what? Why not? You come into my life like an ebola virus. Damn cuckoo in the nest tryna teef up my sister love.

Bo You're right I'm tryna steal your sister! You're choking her off at the root 'cause you don't give her a chance to be herself.

Ree Bo –

Tree Apple ain't fall all that far from the family tree and you stamped through with your rotten mother's rottenness.

Bo Who named you judge and jury miss most high, like you don't bleed once a month, what?

Tree You gonna be bleeding in a minute.

Bo Don't ever bring up my mum again. Understand? I will take your eyes, Tree, I swear to God.

Tree So your creepy mum with her dirt-caked fingernails left some scars on you 'cause she loved crack more than you, well, here's a great big boo hoo hoo for you, how very sorrowful and sad your little life has been.

Bo (*overlap from 'loved crack'*) Stop for one second and think on what iss like to know that your own blood carryin on like you a pariah! Think that wouldn't hurt? Think again.
    I may well have inherited some compulsions and some behaviours from my mother that ain't all that wholesome, yeah, I like getting high and I like getting into scraps and I don't understand why I do it but I do it. And I say so what? Why you ain't never extended a hand to me? Why?

Bo
    Every time you appear you just grief up the family.
    Mine and Ree's mother . . .
    She's in the ground.
    She died young.
    And thass causa
    You

Ree Hey, Tree . . .

Tree Oban.

Bo What about Oban?

Ree Not Oban, sis.

Tree When you juss rock up on the doorstep 'cause your mum couldn't cope. Mum brought you along 'cause it

was the Christian thing to do. But you wrecked Oban
for us.

Ree Please.

Tree Wrecked it.

You swore at the locals and you spat at the pensioners.
That Oban light, that soft light . . . you tainted that
for her.
  And you stole that thing round your neck.

Bo (*suddenly weak*) No I never . . .

Tree That was Mum's. Grandma's first, then Mum's.
Supposed to be Ree's next.

Ree You're upsetting her.

Tree But you crept into her room and took it out the
drawer and stole it.

Bo Your mum gimme this to tell me what a good girl
I been up there.

Tree She went mad looking for it. Hair falling out kinda
mad. Made her ill looking for it. And wouldn't believe it
was you. Would rather blame me than you. I TOOK
THE LICKS! FOR YOU! MUM DASHED MY VIOLIN
AGAINST THE WALL! Smashed it. Handed me the
brock-up violin and told me thass what I get. All on me.
Causa you and your lying ways. She felt sorry for you
and pitied you because your mum was –

Ree Stop.

Bo What, am I diseased or summink? What? What is so
terrible about me that I don't deserve love? Am I that
low?

Tree Yes.

Bo
You did everything you can
To make me feel like I'm shit, like I'm nothing

Tree
You ARE shit
You ARE nothing

Bo Why you wanna hurt me like that?

Tree I don't wanna hurt you.

Beat.

I wanna kill you.

She sings.

Hey sister guess what
Yo think you're clever you're not
You're a liar, a faker, a manipulator
I see through you

Bo
Hey Sister I see
How high and mighty you be
And I'm done with pretending
that you can be friends
I see through you

Bo / Tree
Hate is stronger than stronger than
Hate is stronger than stronger
Hate is stronger than stronger
Hate is stronger than stronger than
Blood

Ree
This can't be right
Please don't fight

Bo
    All you're tryna control
    Everything, takes its toll
    And your weakness is blinding
    Ain't no way of hiding you're trash

Tree
    All your tryna impress
    Can't stay put you're a mess
    Don't you dare wrap up
    Ree try to take her from me
    I see through you.

Bo / Tree
    Hate is stronger than stronger than
    Hate is stronger than stronger than
    Hate is stronger than stronger than
    Hate is stronger than stronger than
    Blood

Ree
    This won't get us anywhere
    Please stop
    Blood is thicker than thicker than
    Blood is thicker than water

Tree Summink unholy boutchou.
    The addiction. The promiscuity
    The urge in you to destroy goodness.
    All you bring to the world . . .
    Is Death. And I will Never.
    Ever. Call you sister.

    Bo exits in tears.

Come back here! I ain't finished tellin yuh what a slag
you are.

Ree (*sings*)
    Family against family
    Always ends up unhappily

And me trapped in the centre of a war
Can't go outside, can't close the door
Can't you just let this one go
Can't we just give her a place she calls home
A side to her you haven't seen
Don't be so harsh, don't be so mean

Family against family
Tragedy upon tragedy
Put down your guard, sis
Don't be so hard, sis
Extend a love to those who need
Let's unify, sis
Let's pacify, sis

Tree
    She ain't no good, sis,
    Don't have to do this.

Ree
    Love ain't a word,
    Love is a deed
    Family against family
    Let's not end unhappily

Tree
    You're my only sis
    And I love you to bits
    And this other sis ain't a sis
    Juss a manipulative bitch
    And you the only one can't see it
    She put some venom in you
    Poisoned up your mind
    She put some vengeance in you
    This love has made you blind
    And now you hiding things from me
    Secretive and furtive
    Make up your mind what you want to be

Don't waste no time, it's urgent
Cause this girl got the whiff of sulphur about her
The whiff of sudden death about her

And I tell ya 'cause I love you
Don't let this madness mug you
You're my only sis
And I love you to bits
And this other sis ain't a sis
Juss a manipulative bitch
She's the gun and you're the bullet
Simple, sis, nothing else to it

Always been a bad kid since she was young
She's the gun and you're the bullet
Simple, sis, nothing else to it
One day you'll regret what you have done
'Cause that girl has a heart thass beating to destroy
And she's deceiving you like you're her little toy
You my only sis
But this devil's kiss
Will lead to sadness
Not just for you but for me also

Where is your self-love?
Where is your integrity?
Ainchou got no sense of who you are?
Ainchou got no sense of what you're worth?
Might as well tattoo 'Victim' right across your forehead
Thass what Bo seeing you as, sis
Thass what the world seeing you as.

You know you sometimes get all mopey and ask me how
come I don't spend more time with you? Iss because
spending time with you is –
    Depressing.
    Depressing as Hell Itself. 'Cause you ain't growing
right.

47

Ree I know what you think a' me, you think I ain't got identity. You think I can't think for myself and you're wrong. You know what I am, sis? I'm loyal. Not smart like you, maybe, but look what all that smartness has done for you. Made you cold. Made you selfish. I see how you looking at me and Bo when we're juss gassing and catching jokes, you lookin like us like we juss shit in our own knickers, pure distaste beaming outchour eyes. And yes, our sister can get a little wild and yes she get herself into predicaments but you know what, she knows how to sit wid a person when they're feeling blue like me.

And she can dish out some wisdom from her breast if the situation calls for it. And she's funny too. Makes me laugh like I'm gonna piss myself. When was the last time you buss a joke?

Ree exits.

Tree Lemme tell yuh sum'un. Not talking is exhausting! Sulking and stropping can put you in a box. Stepping out the gaff now 'cause I'm tired of my own war. Nice night. Truth be told I'm walking and looking for a way to climb down and make some peace, but the pride in my chest blocking my breathing. And thass why I don't clock the car purring up behind me and the two behemoths sliding out and putting their hands on me and roughing me into the back seat. I don't scream. Fear took my sound from me. They take me to this basement dungeon thing under a pub.

A metal chain hanging down from the ceiling.
    A big meat hook at the end, suspended 'bout head-height.
    Black with dried blood.
    People have died in this room.
    Died begging.
    Died slow.

Is that –?
    Yes
    The nightmare coming true.
    Duvivier.
    Immense.
    Duvivier bigger than you can imagine sitting there
sucking on some *moules marinière* and giving me the
death-ray stare.

Duvivier looking at me like he's tryna work out which
part of me to slice from my body first And some fountain
of courage opens up inside me and I say if this is
summink to do with my sister then it don't matter what
you do to me I ain't telling you where she is. I tell him
plain soldier that even though I loathe my sister like
racist oppression I would never, ever give her up.
    Shock myself, like . . . Flipping jellyfish sister of
mine . . . Like, she's part of me, y'know? The bitch is part
of me. I mean . . . I don't even know where she is, but I'm
still refusing to G her up. And I swear I'm ready. Ready
to back up my invective. Ready to die. And there's one
big long-ass silence while he's looking at me and I feel
like he's actually stopped the clocks from ticking . . .
Duvivier knows I'm being truthful because those eyes will
not countenance a subterfuge and he thinking for a while
before he says to me . . .
    Well he gotta take whass his from me one way of the
other.

I got the keys to my stinking work and this particular
night they got the wages and the takings all up in the
safe. Dressed in black. Bandana across my face. Torchlit.
Thinking how easy it is to lose who you are when the
wall pressing up against your back. Grab the sacks of
money and them too-rude pound coins saying, oy,
whassis, we're sleeping and me telling 'em shut up you
got a new home.

49

I put that two and half thousand quid in Duvivier's paw with my own sweaty hands and ask him if we're square.

We're square, he says.

Like, no more terrifying visits and no more being bundled in a car? No more, he says.

What about my sister? She safe?

Which one?

Both.

They're safe, as things stand.

Just as I'm 'bout to get the eff outta there, he calls me back and my knees knocking straight away. Sez he 'members our old dear was his postman/woman whatever bringing him his letters in the morning and then seeing her on the door and he's sorry to hear she passed on . . . Juss for a second I can see summink in him.

Difference between being demonic and being an actual Demon.

Drizzly dawn never looking so good.

And when I wake my sister up she straight kissin her teeth and don't wanna talk until I break down my night to her.

Ree Yuh lie!

Tree If I lie, I die.

Ree He don't wanna murk us no more?

Tree We are officially a murk-free zone, sistren.

Ree Thass –
Thass well good.
But I'm still proper vex widjuh.

Tree Lissen sis . . . I reckon I been a bit like . . . well, ain't been all that understanding . . . most probly been a bit of a –

Ree Hard-faced cow?

Tree Tough on you.

Ree Thass one way a' putting it.

Tree But, well
  This life
  Boy.
  Yuh find y'self some places boy.
  I –
  Sis –
  Lissen yeah.
  One thing I kinda grasping now.
  With all this dramatics and family pyrotechnics and ting
  Is that iss juss *long*
  And we got a *bond*
  And thass some cherishable shit 'cause some madman
can murk you in a basement,
  Some disease can devour you like it did Mum,
  Some sorta unresolved ting can keep you carrying on
bizarre like Bo,
  And none a that is anything but a squander, sis.

She sings.

It's time to reconcile
After parting for a while
Sweep up the broken glass after the fight
It's alright

Hardness doesn't suit you
And crying just won't soothe you
The only thing that will is unity
You and me

I want us to be sisterly
I want us to be sisterly
I want us to be sisterly
Won't you be sisters with me

Guns, triggers and bullets

Now no one has to pull it
We are liberated, we are free
You and me

I want us to be sisterly
I want us to be sisterly
I want us to be sisterly
Won't you be sisters with me

There've been times when
The world was tumbling around us, oh
And I've always been
Around to shelter from the storm and you
May not need me
To be the mountain that I want to be
But I still need you
To be my best friend, my one and only (*Times* 2.)

Ree
We can still be sisterly
We can still be sisterly (*Times* 4).

Bo Iss a funny thing but while I'm running around
looking over my shoulder is actually when I take the time
to reflect on my shit, like.

And I reckon most of whass pushing me forward and
holding me back at the same time is shame. Shame that
my family life is a holocaust. Feeling like iss my fault
somehow that there's so much hurt flying around. Shame
that my old mum could never give love me like she
s'posed to. All these thoughts swirling round in me while
my body's running. Ain't even in any direction juss
forward motion dynamic.

Then I'm like hold up I'm like running away from
summink and thass not the one, I'm a start running
toward summink . . .

Running toward what though?

Running down the street, running running running . . .

Running all the way up to Oban.

Swear down, I ran. For days no sleep just run. Right state when I got there, but . . . put it this way, I'd a been in a worse state if I'd stayed.

The big thing that I know I gotta do is clean myself of this cocaine money. I have completely wrecked everything and now I gotta put things right.

Sold the batch in one sitting for a lotta dough, a lotta dough. And now the money bundled up in this Fred Perry sports bag juss staring at me like reproachful, like.

You know what the money saying?

The money saying 'Is this what iss all about? Juss us sitting in a sports bag? What about them sisters of yours?'

I say, 'But I can't have loved them to treat them like I did.'

And the money says, 'You love them more than your body can contain – look how sad-sack you are since you leff them in peril like dat.'

And by now I'm sick a' debating with paper cash so I pull up the zip, even though the money still muttering summink.

I lean down to the bag and whisper through the zipper, 'I'm getting rid a' you before you make me too mad.'

Tree Mad early when the postman ring our bell. I'm coming down yampi-eye and hair askew but baseball bat in one hand and hammer in the other just in case someone wants to get into it.

Package.

Bomb?

Unwrap it keeping my head back.

Boy . . .

Whass dis now?

Violin.

No note.

No need.

That flipping girl . . .

Ree Tree! What the heck! A violin!
Who sendjuh this?

Tree You know who sent this still.

Ree Iss beautiful. Go on, play summink.

Tree Even this gift makes me mad 'cause I know where
she got the money from.

Ree A wha di –? Tree, if you knock this thing back on
accounta that shtuppid high horse you high-horsing on
then I will call upon Zeus to smite your arse. Serious.

Tree We both know where this comes from.

Ree Scotland, from the postcode.

Tree Murder money. Devil money.

Ree Whassat gotta do with this piece of musical
equipment right here? This violin ain't know nothing
'bout none a that.

Tree Tainted money, sis.

Ree So cleanse it.

Tree Uh. . .

Ree Uh uh uh. . . let it all go and accept what she's given
you. We ain't never gonna see that girl again. Understand?
And you can dress it up and front it out but thass a loss,
sis. Deep sense of loss. And wherever our sister is – *our
sister* – she's sent this thing to you as a great big gigantic
gesture and if you take it back 'cause you too squeamish
and prissy prim then you'll look back and regret that
thing forever. You ain't Jane flipping Austen, sis. Take
this thing and make some sounds on it and shut the frick
up about it.

    Pause.

Tree . . . I ain't *always* on a high horse . . .

Ree Don't wanna hear it, sis. New dawn. Understand?
New sheriff up in this ting.

Tree Hm.

Ree You're bloody right 'hm'. You're taking it.

Tree Think you tough all of a sudden.

Ree Don't test me.

Tree It *is* nice . . .

Ree Okay then.

Tree Okay then.

Ree (*to audience*) I ain't never spoken to nobody like I
spoke to Tree when I spoke to her like that and it felt
proper nice! Like my feet root through the floor and my
voice a river. Where that come from?

Like it or not, it come from Bo. Say what you want
and her imperfections pretty easy to see, but I reckon I
took some of her strength and swallowed it into me. Iss a
way of keeping her alive, I guess . . . not that I think she's
dead, I *know* she ain't dead, but keeping her close,
keeping her . . . keeping her in the family.

Tree She got me doing criminality and me never so much
as teef a Snickers bar in my life! I sullied my soul for that
wretch-girl.

And yet . . .

I'm glad – well glad ain't right, but – I'm at peace with
what I did – ripping off my workplace – because even
though iss a wrongness, it juss illuminated what I was
keeping hidden . . .

I'm only gonna admit this once, but . . .

That flipping girl got me flooded with bloody
tenderness And yearning and –

Ugh.

Why we ended up here?

We should be . . .

We should be . . .

I dunno, like under a duvet eating ice cream together, painting each other's nails or shit, some bollocks like that.

I dunno.

And instead, I ain't never gonna set my eyes on her again and thass a wrench, like, thass a, like, a lifelong keloid.

Flipping girl.

Got me messing up my mascara.

Could kill her if I saw her.

Flipping girl.

Bo Took a long time for the old fishermen to gimme a shot on the boats. But I proved myself. I'm a good fisherman/woman/whatever. I don't rattle and I don't complain, even when the old men make me clean the cages in the rain. First time on them rough rough seas boy I'm 'bout to heave up my gorge and I'm reaching down to grab the cage fulla crab and that –

Damn necklace.

Their mum's necklace that caught all that conflict twixt the three of us –

Slips right off my frickin neck and into the drink.

Watch it slither around then sink to the depths.

First I'm horrified but then it feels like I've had a boil lanced like I can walk straight first time in years. Juss hope some mermaid catch hold of it and wear it with love.

Keep my head down, of course. Used to be that every floorboard creak had me bounce up looking for escape . . . but coupla years into it and I'm pretty sure I'm safe.

Pretty sure . . .

Tree Music college hard, yes! Like they wanna make it as joyless as possible to see if you really want it. But I'm doing good and meeting up with some people who can really play. Writing some different shit now. And that flipping girl . . . Every time I scrape that bow I think of . . . Uh well . . . Bo. Flipping girl.

Ree So here's how I see it.

Mum passed away and thass what brings Bo back to us.

Bo getting on bizarre and thass made us face the crucible.

And thass how I'm getting to know what I need to know about myself. Faced up to a truth not so long after this . . . Here's me tryna hold the sisters together and me not even really and truly not even knowing who this chick is thass staring at me in the looking glass, y'know? So this is when I juss duss . . . Tree weren't happy but . . . can't be living my life seeking approval and putting everyone else's needs in front of my own needs . . . even though I dunno what I need just yet. Otherwise I'm some sorta sister in perpetuity, like, juss being a sister is all there is to me and thass . . . thass a shame, y'know? More than a shame. Thass . . .

Thass juss not me.

Road stretching out and the sky kinda nice. Summink gonna happen. Soon as I know where I'm headed.

Bo Cold up here and the locals kinda surly sometimes. But the light . . .

Makes you breathe.

And the solitude has it's pleasures. Maybe best for me to be alone.

Just the light and the sea and thass all there is for me.

All Three (*sing*)
Sun burns and blisters me
Nothing like we sisters three
And I miss that old sweet sound
Of laughter all around
Three, three, three three, three, three

Through trouble, toil and strife
Watch over sisters' life
And far as we may be
My family lives in me
Three, three, three

Times 4.